AN
IS...

Written by Linda McNabb

Illustrated by Mike Cressy

For Elaine

CONTENTS

CHAPTER ONE

If at First You Don't Succeed...

It seems like ten years ago since I entered my first contest, but it couldn't be – I just turned ten in January. It might seem so long because I've never won anything. It's so unfair!

Today was going to be different though. I just knew it. I raced ahead of Mom at the supermarket and headed for the magazines.

"Come on, Erin. The May issue of *Kid Stuff* is here," I shouted to my best friend.

"What's the prize in this contest, Alicia?" Erin asked excitedly when she had caught up.

"Umm... a couple of movie tickets," I said, thumbing through the magazine.

Jenni, my rotten little sister, came up behind us. "Did you win? Will you take me?"

There weren't any kids her age in our neighborhood, and Mom always insisted that I let her join in with me and my friends. What a pain! Who wants their seven-year-old sister hanging around all the time?

"No way," I said without even thinking about it or looking up from my magazine. Where was that list of contest winners? "Besides, you wrote all over my last magazine. Don't try to deny it. You're the only one who puts a little heart over each *i* and *j* instead of a dot."

"There's the list, Alicia. You just went past it," cried Erin, jumping up and down with excitement.

A few grown-ups glared at us and looked for our parents, but I didn't care. I was about to win my first contest. I flipped back the page and ran my finger down the list of winners. I was so excited that I missed my name and had to start at the top again. Rats! I missed it again. I started at the top for a third time, but when I reached the bottom I realized with horror that my name wasn't even there. I hadn't won!

"Well? Did you win, Alicia?" Mom came up next to me as I closed the magazine with a heavy sigh.

"No, not this time." I threw the magazine into the shopping cart. Maybe they had just forgotten to put my name on the list. They might send me a letter to tell me I'd won after all. No… what was I thinking? Maybe I should stop entering contests.

"Hey, Alicia," Erin said as she picked up the magazine out of the cart and looked at the cover. "There's a contest in here to win a trip to Disneyland."

"There is?" I ran to her and looked. Sure enough, first prize was a family trip to Disneyland. "Wow, I've got to enter that."

"Well, don't forget to take us with you when you win," said Mom, laughing as she pushed the cart toward the checkout counter.

On the way home Erin and I read the rules of the contest. Jenni was trying to see what we were doing the whole time. The good news was that it only took a few minutes to get home. I wanted to get rid of Jenni and fill out the entry form right away.

"Oh no you don't." Mom stood in front of us as Erin and I tried to race off to my bedroom. "Please help unload the groceries first, girls."

By the time we had put away all the food, Rachel and Ashleigh were knocking on the front door. The four of us had started a club a few weeks ago, and today we were supposed to be having our first meeting. We didn't have a name for the club yet, because we couldn't agree on one.

"No sisters allowed," I said as Jenni tried to follow us to my room. "Hey, that could be the name of our club."

"I don't have a sister," Erin pointed out. "Just my older brother, Daniel."

"Neither do I," Ashleigh added. "Just my big brother, Jason the Giant Mouth."

We all groaned, and I shut the door in front of Jenni. The four of us sat and looked at each other for a few minutes. What were you supposed to do in a meeting anyway?

"Let's play cards," Erin suggested, and we all eagerly agreed.

We had barely finished dealing the cards when I looked out the window and saw Jenni at the mailbox. She always got the mail. Everyone had long since stopped trying to beat her to the mailbox, but she still ran as if someone was racing her.

"Hey, Alicia, there's a letter for you," Jenni called sweetly. With a wicked grin, she waved the letter at me through the open window.

Just as I reached out to grab it, Jenni disappeared.

CHAPTER TWO

I Must Be Dreaming

Where had that little squirt gone? Jenni was always playing tricks, and this one was just as annoying as all the others!

Suddenly, her face popped back up at my bedroom window.

"Hand me that letter right now," I ordered, thrusting my hand back through the open window. Who could have sent it? I squinted at the letter, trying to see whose writing was on the front, but Jenni had it facing the wrong way. Maybe it was from my pen pal, Kim, in Australia.

"OK," Jenni said, holding the letter just out of my reach, "but first you have to let me into your club."

"Forget it!" I replied as I heaved myself onto the windowsill, grabbing for the letter. What a rotten little sister!

"Then you can't have your dumb letter," Jenni said with a sweet smile. The next thing I knew, she was running down the front walk.

"Come back with that," I yelled through the open window, but she didn't stop. I quickly dashed past my friends and down the hallway. "I'll get you, Jennifer Rose!"

I raced to the front yard, but there was no sign of her. I went around to the back of the house, but she wasn't there either.

"Are you looking for something?" Jenni leaned over the deck railing and waved the letter again before she disappeared inside.

"Mom! Mom!" I yelled. I'd had enough of that little rat. I ran into the kitchen and found Mom making iced tea. "Jenni took my letter."

"Which letter, sweetheart?" Mom asked calmly, picking up the letter from the kitchen table. "This one?"

"She ran off with it," I gasped, almost snatching the letter right out of her hand.

"Well, don't you think you should have let her into your club?" asked Mom.

"Oh Mom," I complained, looking at the writing on the front of the envelope. I didn't recognize it. It wasn't Kim's writing. It looked more like an adult's. I carried the letter back to my bedroom and shut the door before Jenni could try to come in.

"Who's the letter from?" Rachel asked as she picked up her pile of cards.

"I don't know," I replied, carefully ripping it open. My heart was beating so loudly I was sure everyone in the room would be able to hear it. Maybe the magazine had written to me after all!

"Come on, it's your turn," Ashleigh said, pushing my cards toward me.

"It's from the store down the street," I said, looking at the name at the top of the page. I read the first few words and nearly fell over. They were: "A big congratulations to our winner, Alicia Montoya!"

I blinked twice, rubbed my eyes, and read on. "You have won first prize in our yearly Two-Minute Toy Grab. Please come to the store on..."

"I won! I won!" I yelled at the top of my lungs. I had finally won something. I couldn't remember entering the contest, but that was nothing new. I must have, or I wouldn't have won, would I?

"What did you win?" Erin grabbed the letter from me and read it out loud. I was too busy daydreaming to pay attention.

"Who are you going to take with you?" Rachel asked.

"Huh?" I snapped back to reality. "Take with me? You can all come and watch if you want to," I said with a gigantic grin on my face. I had won!

"No, I mean the letter says that you have to take one person to help you grab the toys." Erin quickly pointed out the last two lines of the letter.

I hadn't read that far, so I took the letter back. It was true. I had to pick one friend to help me. I frowned and looked at the three friends sitting on my bed. Who was I going to choose?

CHAPTER THREE

The Race Is On

The rest of our club meeting didn't go well, to say the least. Everyone wanted to be my helper at the Toy Grab. Finally, Mom came in and sent everyone home. She wasn't too happy with the way we were all arguing.

The next day at school was even worse. A bunch of kids had heard about the contest, and they all wanted to help me grab toys.

"But I was in your class last year..."

"I invited you to my birthday party..."

Enough! Who would have thought that winning a contest could possibly cause so much trouble?

A week later, one day before the Toy Grab, I still hadn't picked a helper, and it was driving me nuts. All kinds of kids – most claiming to be my best friend – had been hanging around my house all day. I had to choose someone, and I had to do it now.

"OK," I said, standing up quickly and going out the front door. My ever-present group of followers gathered around me. "I am going to pick someone."

"How?" said a voice from the group.

Suddenly, I had an idea. "You can all race for it," I said.

"As in running races?" asked Erin, looking very puzzled.

"No, downhill, on pieces of cardboard," I said, walking down the slope next to my house, which had a creek at the bottom of it. "I'll stand down here, and the first person to reach me is the winner."

"Cool," an older, deeper voice said. I looked to see who it belonged to. Daniel!

"No way. No older boys are allowed in this race," I announced loudly, knowing that it was too late.

"Tough! You should have said that earlier," said Jason, Daniel's best friend. "You can't just change the rules like that!"

I glared at Daniel and Jason, but they just laughed at me. It didn't matter if either of them won – there was no way I would take them anyway. The first kid my age to make it down the hill would be the winner, I thought to myself.

"Meet me here in an hour with a piece of cardboard," I said loudly so that everyone would hear. Then I went inside. "I wish I'd never won that contest," I muttered.

Jenni laughed at me as she colored with crayons in the middle of the living-room floor. Why hadn't she asked to come and help? Oh well, who could understand little sisters?

Before I knew it, the hour was up, and the whole hill next to my house was lined with kids. Everyone had a piece of cardboard, and some of those pieces looked like they wouldn't make it all the way down. I walked to the bottom of the hill with an old white dish towel that I was going to use to start the race.

Looking up at the row of determined faces, I suddenly knew that this race was a bad idea. Someone could easily get hurt. I quickly looked up toward the house and was pleased

to see that Jenni was watching from the deck. Mom would ground me forever if Jenni broke her arm again. Twice this year was enough.

There had to be a better way than this to pick someone. I raised my hands and yelled, "The race is called off!"

Unfortunately, one of my hands held the white dish towel, of course. A huge cheer went up as a whole pack of cardboard riders sped toward me. Oh no, this definitely wasn't a good idea.

Daniel and Jason were in the lead and heading straight for me. If they didn't change direction soon, they would crash right into me. It was all happening so fast!

"Get out of the waayyy!" Jason yelled as he picked up even more speed.

I looked around to find a safe place to run to. There wasn't one. I had my back to the

creek and nowhere to go. Jason was getting close, and I jumped quickly to the side to avoid him. That was a bad move. I had jumped right in front of Daniel. He hit me square in the leg, and I fell on top of him.

"Stop! Stop!" I yelled. Daniel and I were skidding out of control on his cardboard, and I could see the creek getting closer and closer.

"I can't," shouted Daniel. "Wow, this is really cool!"

Then we landed in the creek.

"All right! I won!" Daniel bragged as he came up out of the water.

"You did not. I said no older boys!" I yelled. By then, everyone else had reached the bottom, and they were all gathered around, staring at Daniel and me.

"You've got a stick on your head," Daniel said. He laughed and shook the water off himself, spraying everyone around him.

I reached up, tugged the stick out of my hair, and pulled myself up onto the side of the bank. Who had been the first kid my age? I hadn't seen who had won. Oh no. Did this mean we would have to do it all over again? I thought as hard as I could.

"Here, I'll help you up, Alicia," said Erin, reaching down to give me a hand.

I put one foot down on the grass, but when I tried to stand up, it felt as if pieces of sharp metal were inside my leg.

"Owww!" I yelled as I collapsed onto the ground. "My leg!"

Just then, Dad came charging down the hill, and he didn't look happy. I wasn't happy either. Suddenly, everyone realized this wasn't a good place to be right now, and they all took off. I tried to stand again and collapsed in horrible pain. My leg was broken.

CHAPTER FOUR

Just My Luck!

"I hate boys," I mumbled as I slowly woke up and looked around the room. Everything was bright and clean and smelled like disinfectant. There were two more children lying in the other beds in the room. Where was I? A few horrible seconds later, I remembered. I was in the hospital because stupid old Daniel had broken my leg!

It still felt like I had pieces of metal in my leg. In fact, the doctor told me he'd almost had to put some metal pins in my bone to help it heal. I guess I'd been lucky. Well, sort of. Just wait until I got my hands on Daniel!

"Mom…," I called out, feeling suddenly alone and frightened. "Snowy."

Snowy was my stuffed polar bear. I'd had her since I was a little kid. Now, I know I'm a little too old to be so attached to a silly stuffed animal, but I can't help it. I mean, I was stuck in this hospital in a strange bed, and, well, Mom understood me...

"How are you feeling, sweetheart?" Mom's face appeared at the door, and she came in holding Snowy. I took my bear and held her closely. Snowy made me feel much better.

"OK, I guess," I replied.

It wouldn't be so bad. I could get everyone to sign my cast, and I wouldn't have to go to gym class for weeks. I'd also have tons of time to play with the new toys I would get from the Toy Grab. "I just want to get home so that I can go to the Toy Grab tomorrow," I continued.

"Yes... we'll need to talk about that," Mom said slowly.

I could tell she was hiding something, and I knew it wouldn't be good news.

"We'll talk about it later, OK? Right now, some of your friends are waiting outside. I'll tell them to come in." Mom disappeared, and Erin, Rachel, and Ashleigh came in.

"We brought you some candy," Erin said, putting a half-empty crumpled bag on the table next to my bed. "We had some while we were waiting."

"Sorry about the Toy Grab," Rachel said as she sat on the edge of my bed.

"Do you want us to go and watch so we can tell you what happens?" asked Ashleigh.

"But I'll be there. What are you talking about?" I tried to sit up, but my stiff cast got in the way, and I had to lie back down. What a pain!

"But your mom said you weren't going," Erin objected. "Jenni's…"

I could see that Erin had said something she wasn't supposed to because she put her hand over her mouth and turned bright red.

"What *about* Jenni?" I demanded, wishing I could sit up. I didn't sound too forceful when I was flat on my back.

"She's going to go to the Toy Grab in your place," said Mom as she came back into the room and stood at the end of the bed.

"Jenni? But that was *my* prize! Why can't *I* go?" Life wasn't fair at all. I had finally won something and my rotten little sister was going to get all the fun.

"You won't be able to put any pressure on your leg for a while. It will hurt too much." Mom tried to explain it to me, but I didn't really want to listen.

"I'm sure Jenni will grab toys for both of you," she said, trying to soothe me.

"Why can't one of my friends go in my place?" I asked. Jenni would pick baby toys, not the cool ones I wanted.

"Sorry, the toy store owner said the main contestant had to be a family member. Would you rather your father or I went instead?" Mom asked. She knew what I would say.

"No." Of course not! If I had to choose, then Jenni was better. At least she would get toys, not just "educational" stuff. "It's still not fair," I said.

"I know," Mom agreed, smoothing the hair from my face.

"I'm tired," I said grumpily. I pulled the blankets up over my head.

"I'll come and pick you up tomorrow," promised Mom, leading the three girls out.

The rest of the afternoon was boring, but the night was worse. I thought hospitals were supposed to be quiet places. Every time I'd ever visited one, Mom had told me to talk quietly and not to run. But all night long, either one of the other kids in the ward was crying or a nurse was walking up and down the hall. Talk about noisy!

"What was wrong with the kids who were crying last night?" I asked one of the nurses.

She was wheeling in a big cart with trays for the kids.

"Do you see your bear?" she said, smiling and pointing at Snowy. I held Snowy tighter. "Not everyone has a toy with them to hug when they get lonely or scared."

What an awful thought. I hated to admit it, but that was just how I had felt until Mom had brought Snowy in. I didn't get to talk more with the nurse because she hurried off to deliver the remaining trays. So I sat eating and thinking about the Toy Grab and how unfair it was that I was going to miss it.

Later that day, Mom came to take me home. She had to push me out to the car in a wheelchair. Now I *knew* I wouldn't be walking in the near future!

"Where are we going?" I asked when Mom turned the car in the opposite direction from home. I just wanted to be safe in my house and to shut myself in my room. There was no way I wanted to see Jenni with all her great new toys.

"We just need to make a quick stop on the way," was all Mom would say, and I tried to guess where we were going.

It wasn't until we pulled into the toy store parking lot that I figured it out.

"No way!" I almost yelled. "Isn't it bad enough that I can't be part of the Toy Grab? Now you're going to make me watch Jenni take my place?"

How could Mom do this to me? I wanted to run off, but of course I could barely even move. I had to let Mom help me into the hospital wheelchair she had pulled from the trunk, and then steer me into the toy store.

The store was crowded with people, and Jenni was standing just in front of them with a huge shopping cart.

"I thought you might like to see the person Jenni picked as her partner in the Toy Grab," Mom said as she rolled me toward my sister.

"Why? I'm sure it's her friend Natasha." I pouted and refused to look up.

"Well, it's not. She chose you."

CHAPTER FIVE

Can You Believe It?

"What?" I couldn't believe my ears. My rotten little sister chose me? Then my heart sank. "But I can't walk."

"She's figured all that out," Dad said. Then he scooped me up and put me into the cart. "She'll push and you'll grab!"

I stared at my rotten little sister in disbelief as she grinned at me. Why did she choose me? But there was no time to ask her just then. The store owner pulled out a toy starter's pistol and began the Toy Grab. We were off and running!

"Down to aisle three, Jenni," I shouted as Jenni heaved the cart into motion. She was pretty strong for such a little squirt.

Everyone else was shouting too. How Jenni managed to hear my directions, I'll never know, but she pushed me all around the store before she grabbed a few things for herself. Two minutes doesn't seem like long, but we had the cart packed all over me and still had thirty seconds to go.

Suddenly, an idea came to me, and I pointed Jenni in the direction of the huge wall of stuffed toys.

"Grab two of everything," I yelled, and we both jammed the bears, rabbits, monkeys, and clowns into the gaps in the cart.

BEEP, BEEP, BEEP.

The horn marking the end of the two minutes sounded, and we threw the last toy into the cart. Everyone clapped, and Jenni slowly pushed the overloaded cart back to where we had started. Mom, Dad, Erin, Rachel, and Ashleigh were waiting for us.

"Wow, look at all the toys!" exclaimed Erin. "But why did you grab so many stuffed animals, Alicia?"

"You'll see," I replied as Mom and Dad emptied the cart. I had plans for those toys.

"Can we get a picture?" A woman with a camera stepped forward. The badge on her sweater said she was from the local paper.

This was great! Today wasn't turning out to be so bad after all. I got to be in the Toy Grab, and now I was going to be in the newspaper.

"Let's take a shot with you holding the entry form for the contest, OK?" suggested the photographer.

The store owner came over and handed me the form. As I looked at it, I frowned. It didn't look familiar at all, and I was baffled.

"Smile," the photographer called out, and I pushed the frown away, but it came back as soon as she had snapped my picture.

Something was definitely wrong here. I looked closer at the entry form, and my eyes nearly popped out. My name was on it, but those little hearts were over each *i* and *j*!

"Jenni?" Shocked, I stared at my rotten little sister. Well, maybe I shouldn't call her "rotten" anymore. She had filled out the form with my name on it!

Jenni just smiled back at me, and then she asked quietly, "Can I join your club?"

Before I got a chance to tell her I would be happy to let her join, the photographer wanted me to answer a question.

"Why did you want so many stuffed toys?" she asked.

I smiled. "They're for the children's ward at the hospital. That way, if a little girl or boy forgets to bring their own special toy, the hospital will have something to give them."

The camera flashed again, and everyone clapped and cheered – especially me. Then I leaned over to hug my *awesome* little sister.

From the Author

I was born in England, but I grew up in New Zealand, where I live today with my husband and two daughters. I progressed from telling imaginative stories as a child to writing them down as a teenager. Reading has also been an important part of my life. Sometimes, if you learn through reading about how others deal with the hurdles of life, you don't have to learn the hard way.

Everyone loves to enter contests, and I'm no different, but few of us ever win. Some of us give up trying, but others keep going and eventually become "the winner." The thrill of succeeding at anything in life makes it all worthwhile, but you have to give it a try, or you will never know!

Linda McNabb

If you have enjoyed reading *And the Winner Is...*, read these other *Storyteller* Chapter Books.

The Klutzy Cat
Seiko the Watchdog
The Magic Shoes
How Not to Catch the Moon
Spider and Buffalo
Turtles, Tortoises, and Terrapins
Bats about Bats!

From the Illustrator

While I was growing up, I drew and painted all the time. I had one sister and three brothers. It seems that they – and everybody else! – always had something to say about how much I liked to draw. Over the years, some people have understood my love of art, and some haven't.

I now live near Seattle, the rainiest part of the United States, paint pictures, and try to stay warm and dry in my little house with the help of some hot cocoa.

Mike Cressy